DATE DUE

THE PIT CREW

RACE CAR LEGENDS

COLLECTOR'S EDITION

THE PIT CREW

Tara Baukus Mello

CHELSEA HOUSE
PUBLISHERS

An imprint of Infobase Publishing

The Pit Crew
©2007 by Infobase Publishing

Chelsea House
An imprint of Infobase Publishing
132 West 31st Street
New York NY 10001

ISBN-10: 0-7910-8665-8
ISBN-13: 978-0-7910-8665-0

Library of Congress Cataloging-in-Publication Data
Mello, Tara Baukus.
  The pit crew / Tara Baukus Mello.
    p. cm. – (Race car legends. Collector's edition)
Includes bibliographical references and index.
ISBN 0-7910-8665-8 (hardcover)
1. Automobile racing—Juvenile literature. 2. Pit crews—Juvenile literature.
I. Title. II. Series.
GV1029.M47 2007   796.72—dc22

Chelsea House books are available at special discounts when purchased in bulk quantities for businesses, associations, institutions, or sales promotions. Please call our Special Sales Department in New York at (212) 967-8800 or (800) 322-8755.

You can find Chelsea House books on the World Wide Web at http://www.chelseahouse.com

Series design by Erika K. Arroyo
Cover design by Hierophant Publishing Services/EON PreMedia/Joo Young An

Printed in the United States of America

Bang PH 10 9 8 7 6 5 4 3 2 1

This book is printed on acid-free paper.

All links and Web addresses were checked and verified to be correct at the time of publication. Because of the dynamic nature of the Web, some addresses and links may have changed since publication and may no longer be valid.

CONTENTS

1

IN THE PITS

Winning a car race depends on two things: a car that is in top shape and a driver who can drive that car to the finish line first. No matter how good a driver is, he or she will not be able to win unless the car is in excellent condition.

The people who take care of the cars in a race are on a team called a pit crew. Being in the pit area at a racetrack is the most exciting place to be in car racing, unless you are in the driver's seat, of course. In all types of car racing, the people in a pit crew work behind the scenes to make sure a car is in perfect condition for a race. Each member of the pit crew has a different duty, but all the members must work together to prepare the car properly for the race.

There's a good reason for teamwork in pit crews. Their job isn't just to prepare the cars for a race. They also need to take care of the cars during the race. When a race car driver needs more gasoline, or maybe a tire change, he pulls over for a pit stop where his pit crew is waiting.

In many forms of car racing members of the pit crew practice their pit stop routines again and again to make sure they work on the car as fast as possible on race day. There are many different kinds of car racing, and each has

Matt Kenseth's pit crew demonstrates its skills during the Union 76/ Rockingham World Pit Crew Competition held at the North Carolina Speedway near Rockingham, North Carolina, in November 2002.

its own kind of pit stop routine. For example, in drag racing, drivers zip down a straight track that is one-quarter mile long. The drivers release parachutes from the backs of their cars to help them slow down at the end of the track. Each round of the race lasts only a few seconds. Because each round is so short, drivers don't take pit stops like they do in stock car racing, which takes place on a large oval racetrack. Instead drag racers go to their pit areas between each round. There, the pit crew fixes up the car to make it go faster in the next round. If there has been a minor accident or a mechanical problem during the round, the pit crew must make major repairs on the car. Some drag racing pit crews have replaced whole engines between

Tony Schumacher deploys the parachutes in his Top Fuel dragster after running the fastest quarter-mile speed in Pomona Raceway history on February 12, 2005. Schumacher ran a speed of 334.65 mph at the racetrack in Pomona, California.

rounds. Although there is no way for a drag racing team to practice pit stops as teams do in other types of racing, everyone knows that working quickly means the difference between winning and losing.

WHO'S IN CHARGE?

The person who oversees the pit crew is called the crew chief. On all teams, the crew chief is the person who makes the decisions about what is done to the race car every time it enters the pit area. On some racing teams, the crew chief works on the car along with the crew; on other teams, the crew chief acts only as a supervisor. The crew chief considers many different pieces of information when deciding what to tell his crew to do. He talks to the driver about how the car performed on the track. He examines information from computers that show what was happening to the car during each turn in the race. The chief also takes into consideration the weather and the location and condition of the track. He puts all these pieces of the puzzle together to make decisions about how to improve the car's performance.

Experience is the key to making the right decisions. The longer the crew chief has worked around race cars, the more skilled he is at making the best decisions to help the driver win. That is why no pit crewmember starts out as a crew chief. Crew chiefs must work their way up through the ranks before they get the top position.

THE BUSINESS OF RACING

Today, car racing is big business. Companies give money to car racing organizations in exchange for having their company names displayed on the tracks for fans to see. Larger amounts of prize money have enabled car racing to become a highly technical sport. Crew chiefs often spend more time looking at computer screens than they do looking under the hoods of race cars. Ray Evernham, owner of Evernham Motorsports and former crew chief for NASCAR Cup champion Jeff Gordon, said, "I've had to spend a lot of time reading up on things I should have paid attention to in high school." Understanding the technology behind racing could be the key to getting a job with a pit

Jimmie Johnson's chief engineer, Darian Grubb, watches the action from atop the team's hauler. Because of Grubb's pit experience, he was able to replace Chad Knauss as Johnson's pit crew chief when Knauss was suspended for breaking rules.

crew in the future. Teams now hire engineers and computer specialists to give them the competitive edge they need to win.

JOB-SPECIFIC CREW

Speed is important on the track, and the speed of the pit crew is important in the pit. To ensure that work is done fast, each crewmember has a specific job. For example, in NASCAR racing, there is one person whose job it is to put fuel in the car. In drag racing, one person packs the parachutes that enable the drivers to stop at the end of the quarter-mile. In off-road racing, one person points the driver to the right pit area, often with a flashlight, because many races last into the evening. Each person on the pit crew is equally important because without each member doing his or her job, the driver cannot do his or her best on the track.

Top Fuel driver Melanie Troxel packs a parachute to ready her dragster for the NHRA Mile High Nationals at Bandimere Speedway in Morrison, Colorado, in July 2006.

Crewmember salaries vary greatly. The most inexperienced crewmembers are paid the least. Members with the most experience receive higher salaries. In NASCAR Nextel Cup racing, for example, a pit crewmember can make $30,000 to more than $100,000 per year, depending on the person's experience, which tasks he or she performs in the pit, and the overall success of the team.

Car owner and crew chief Ray Evernham monitors the race from the pit box at the 2005 Sylvania 300 NASCAR NEXTEL Cup race in Loudon, New Hampshire.

Pit crews are generally on the road traveling more than they are at home. In many types of car racing, there is a race nearly every weekend during the racing season. Days are long, at the track and at the team shop where the team meets to practice.

Ferrari driver Michael Schumacher of Germany is cheered by his pit crew as he heads for the finish line to win the 2000 Formula One Grand Prix in Melbourne, Australia. Racing is a team sport, and the pit crew shares in the victory.

Crewmembers sometimes work late into the night, only to report back to work again the next morning. Everyone feels the pressure to win, but people don't join a pit crew just for the possible prize money. The bottom line for every member of the pit crew in every type of car racing is that they love racing. They are willing to spend long hours at work, countless days on the road, and time away from their families in exchange for the feeling they get when they see their team car cross the finish line first.

2

NASCAR RACING

NASCAR racing is one of the most popular sports in the United States today. In 2004, 196 million households watched NASCAR Cup racing events on television. Like baseball's major league, NASCAR has three top-level classes that race nationally—Nextel Cup, Busch, and Craftsman Truck.

In NASCAR racing, there is a wall that separates the racetrack from the lane the drivers pull into on a pit stop. There is another wall that separates the pit crews from the pit lane. Seven crewmembers "go over the wall," or over the barrier that separates the pit crews from the cars as they pull into pit lane. Together, the pit crew performs its duties in a well-practiced performance. Pit crews often practice their pit stops in the race shop several times a week. Some teams practice every day.

HOW THE TEAM WORKS TOGETHER

The crew chief decides when the driver should come into the pit lane. This decision is based on many things, such as how much fuel the car has left, whether the tires need changing, how well the car is performing on the track, and if the race is currently under a yellow **caution flag**.

A pit crewmember heads over the wall to service a car at the Daytona Racetrack.

Each team has a stall on "pit row," the area on the outside of the pit lane. When the driver reaches the pit stall, his pit crew is allowed to jump over the wall that separates the pit stalls from the pit lane. Once the car has stopped, the **jackman**, the front and rear tire changers, and the front and rear tire carriers run around to the passenger side of the car. While the jackman raises the car off the ground, the two tire changers start to take off the tires. Once a tire is off, the tire carriers hand a new tire to the changers, who put it on and tighten the lugs, or bolts, that hold it in place. The process is then repeated on the opposite side of the car.

At the same time, a gasman and a catch-can man refuel the car. The gasman fills the fuel tank using a can that contains 11 gallons of racing gas and which weighs about

80 pounds. The catch-can man's job is to hold a can at the opening of a small vent in the rear of the car to catch any excess fuel. The fuel is then weighed to determine exactly how much fuel was put into the car.

While these seven people are hard at work, several others assist them from behind the wall. Each tire carrier has an assistant who hands a fresh tire over the wall. A second gasman hands a second can of fuel over the wall to the first gasman, who puts the gas in the car. Another person washes the windshield using a squeegee mounted on a long pole. Someone else uses another long pole to pass the driver a drink of water. When the jackman lowers

The jackman raises the car while crewmembers change tires and service the car driven by Tony Stewart during the Ford 400 NASCAR race at Homestead-Miami Speedway, Homestead, Florida, in November 2006.

the car back down after the work is done, the driver heads back out onto the track.

WOMEN ON THE CREW

Nicole Addison and Sara Dykehouse are two crewmembers for the No. 16 Chevy Silverado truck driven by Jack Sprague in the NASCAR Craftsman Truck races. Sprague has won the series championship three times in his career, most recently in 2001. Addison is the rear tire changer for Sprague's car during races and is also the pit crew coordinator at the race shop. She was the first woman to go "over the wall" in NASCAR Craftsman Truck racing.

Sara Dykehouse *(left)* and Nicole Addison at the Lowes Motor Speedway in Charlotte, North Carolina, in May 2005.

Nicole Addison, holding an air gun, is ready for action as a tire changer. Addison is the first woman to go "over the wall" in NASCAR Craftsman Truck racing.

During a race, Addison jumps over the wall as soon as Sprague pulls into the pit stall. She has her air gun in her hand and begins loosening the lugs that hold the tire in

TIMES HAVE CHANGED

In 1960, a racing team named Wood Brothers Racing discovered that they could cut the length of time for some pit stops in half with a bit of effort. In those days, a pit stop in which two tires were changed and the car was refueled lasted about 48 seconds. By practicing pit stops and deciding where each crewmember would be, Wood Brothers reduced the time for this type of pit stop to 23 seconds.

Pit stops also took longer in the 1960s and 1970s because of the equipment crews used. Back then, the jack used to lift the car weighed 80 pounds and took many pumps to raise the car high enough to change the tires. In addition, tire changers used four-prong wrenches instead of high-speed air guns to loosen and tighten the lug nuts. Plus, the gasman had to screw the gas cap on and off by hand, which took even more time.

place. Dykehouse, who is the team's tire specialist, stays behind the wall and holds the hose connected to Addison's air gun, so no one accidentally trips. When Addison and the tire carrier are ready for the second tire, Dykehouse hands the new tire over the wall and takes the old tire.

"When the pit crew is done, that's when my job really begins," says Dykehouse. She takes the old tires and takes many measurements, including checking the tire pressure and which spots on the tire are worn down, and then inputs this information into the computer. The crew chief then looks at the information and makes decisions about what changes to make in the next pit stop. "It fascinates me because tires can have that much effect on the performance," says Dykehouse.

Pit crewmembers check tire wear and record data during a NASCAR race.

EARLY VERSUS MODERN TIMES

Today, the NASCAR teams complete a pit stop in 13 to 18 seconds. But in the beginning of stock car racing, it wasn't unusual for teams to take a minute or more during a pit stop. Often, if the car had to make a pit stop when the rest of the cars were racing, that driver got behind the rest by an entire lap. NASCAR Cup racing was more than 10 years old when a team first realized that they could gain an advantage if they could shorten their pit stops.

Early stock car racing took place in cow pastures and at the beach. Back then, there weren't any rules: Anybody could race against anybody else, driving any type of car they wanted. The sport quickly became popular, and, before long, people paid to come to watch the races. The drivers split the money people paid, the majority of which went to the winner. It didn't take long for stock car racing to become competitive, and soon drivers began to add new parts to their cars to make their engines go faster.

In 1934, Bill France visited Daytona Beach, Florida, and was fascinated by the stock car races that were held on the beach. France found it so exciting that he moved to Florida so he, too, could race. In December of 1947, he held a meeting with other drivers in the area, and they formed the National Association of Stock Car Auto Racing, or NASCAR. The first NASCAR race was held in February of 1948. Half of the track was on the sand of Daytona Beach and the other half was on the street that ran alongside the beach. This race eventually became the Daytona 500, which is shown on national television today.

In the early days of stock car racing, the driver didn't communicate much with his crew once he was on the track. Teams gathered together before the race to decide the strategy, and the only time they could talk was during a pit stop. Because this was not very effective, crewmembers began to use large chalkboards to relay messages to the drivers. Pit crews would write messages on the chalkboard and hold it up as the drivers raced by their pit stalls. Unfortunately, the message board wasn't very effective

Red Farmer's number 61 car flies into the air after hitting a hole while racing on Daytona Beach in 1953.

either. Reading the board meant that drivers had to take their eyes off the racetrack to glance over at the pits and read the sign. In addition, drivers could only respond after they had passed the pits, read the sign, and completed another lap around to the pits again.

To help improve this situation, a simple system of hand signals was created so drivers could send messages to pit crews. If a driver needed tires for the right side of the car, for example, he or she would put two fingers on the roof when passing the pit stall. If the driver needed two tires for the left side, he or she would put two fingers on the door. If the car was overheating, the driver would hold his nose.

Although this was more effective, communication really wasn't much improved until two-way radios

Sara Dykehouse transports a gas can to the pit area in preparation for a race.

(walkie-talkies) were invented. Today, a driver uses a tiny radio that plugs into his or her helmet. To talk to the pit crew, a driver pushes a button on the steering wheel and talks into a microphone mounted in his or her helmet. When pit crewmembers respond, the driver usually hears them clearly through an earpiece, also mounted in the helmet, which is fitted especially for each person's ear.

PREPARING FOR PHYSICAL LABOR

Crewmembers often have one job at the races and a different job at the race shop. Nicole Addison changes tires during the race, but on a typical day at the race shop, she handles all of the aspects of the pit practices in her role as pit crew coordinator. The crew practices for about 90 minutes almost every day they are in the race shop. Addison sets up all the equipment in the practice pit in the morning and then practices stops with the rest of the crew after lunch. Sometimes the pit crew coach has the crew do specific drills to work on one aspect of the pit stops, and others times he has them do 10 full pit stops in a row.

Both Addison's and Dykehouse's jobs require lots of physical labor, and so they are required to stay in shape in order to be on the team. For both women (as well as the rest of the crew), the workday begins at 6:00 A.M. at the gym, where the entire crew exercises as a group. The workouts are specially designed for each crewmember, depending on the muscles they need the most during a pit stop. Both Addison and Dykehouse focus on building arm strength so they can easily carry tires that weigh up to 75 pounds. Addison also focuses on leg exercises that will help her get up quickly, while Dykehouse rides a bicycle to help her legs move faster when she has to run with the tires. "We are really athletes," says Addison. "It's important to be in good shape and healthy to have the strength for the work."

3

☗☗☗☗☗☗

DRAG RACING

In the time that it takes you to read this sentence, a Top Fuel dragster covered the length of a football field.

Speed is what makes all types of car racing exciting. Whether the racers are on dirt or asphalt, racing in a circle, on the street, or in a straight line, it is the roar of the car's engine zooming by that causes a fan's heart to skip a beat. Of all the types of racing, drag racing is the fastest. Professional drag racers can go more than 300 miles per hour in the quarter-mile race. The entire race often lasts for only about four seconds.

In drag races, two cars race side-by-side on a short track. Racers are matched in pairs and race against each other. The drivers with the faster times in their pairs progress to the next round of competition. The slower driver in each pair is eliminated. When there are only two competitors left, the racer with the faster time wins the competition.

There are four professional classes in drag racing: Top Fuel, Funny Car, Pro Stock, and Pro Stock Motorcycle. Top Fuel is the fastest class, wherein racers drive rear-engine dragsters. Funny Cars, which make up the next fastest class, are basically front-engine dragsters with fiberglass

Morgan Lewis and Bruce Litton race Top Fuel dragsters during the CARQUEST Auto Parts NHRA Winternationals at Auto Club Raceway in Pomona, California, in February 2006.

bodies. Funny Cars resemble passenger cars, such as the Ford Mustang or Pontiac Trans-Am, although they are shorter and have long noses and fat tails. The term *Funny Car* goes back to the 1960s when drag racers took stock racing cars and moved the rear wheels forward, raised the car's front end (or nose), and made other changes that made the car look funny. People referred to them as Funny Cars, and the name stuck. Funny Cars have a **supercharger** that sticks up through the hood, and the driver sits where the rear seat would be in a regular car. Funny Cars don't have doors. Instead, the body must be lifted up in the front in order for the driver to enter. Pro Stock is the class of racing cars that most closely resembles today's street cars. Then there are Pro Stock cars, which are the exact length and width of the cars after which they are modeled. Instead of being made of steel, certain parts, such as the hood, front fenders, and rear deck, are replaced with lightweight versions, often made of fiberglass. The Pro Stock Motorcycles look a bit like today's sport motorcycles, with the addition of a "wing" with extra wings for stability.

Before a drag race, the pit crew drives a truck or a van that tows the race car to the starting line. When a driver's turn comes, the engine is started and the driver does a **burnout**. Smoke billows off the tires. This heats the

A pit crewmember lifts the body of John Force's Funny Car during a pit stop at the NHRA Auto Club finals in November 2005.

John Force, celebrating a "Quarter Century on the Quarter Mile", does a burnout to set up for his race.

rubber on the tires and gives the car **traction** as it heads down the track. The rear tires are made of a special rubber that is soft and gummy and allows them to grip the track.

After the burnout, the driver makes a practice run, called a **dry-hop**, partway down the track. The driver then has to drive backward to the starting line. It is important that the car is straight at the starting line, so a crewmember stands in front of the car and directs the driver while he or she backs up. Once the driver backs up all the way, the crewmember directs the driver to pull forward to the starting line, where there is an electronic beam that starts a timer when the driver leaves the line. Once the drivers are in position, a race official called a starter activates the

TRI-COLORED TREE

The Christmas tree is an electronically controlled system of yellow and green lights mounted on a tall pole between the two racing lanes, just past the starting line. At the top of the pole, two yellow lights flash a signal to the driver that his or her car is near the starting line. A second set of yellow lights

THE 1950s

A "starter" leaps into the air to wave a flag to start a stock car drag race in the 1950s.

Christmas tree. If the driver leaves the starting line before the green light, the red light comes on and the driver is disqualified from the race. At the end of the quarter-mile, the electronic beam stops the timer and instantly flashes the time and the speed of each vehicle onto a large screen for the spectators to see.

DRAG RACING HISTORY

Drag racing wasn't always this high-tech. In the beginning, there was simply a person who waved a flag to signal "go," and a person who timed the race with a stopwatch. The first drag races were run on dry lakebeds in the 1930s. Racers drove their Model T and Model A Fords turns on when the car is ready for its run. These are called the staging lights. Once the cars are staged, five yellow countdown lights flash on from top to bottom. Four-tenths of a second after the last yellow light turns on, the green light flashes. The green light is the driver's signal to go.

2006

This Top Fuel dragster's signal to go is when the Christmas tree's green light flashes.

to the racecourse and stripped off certain parts, such as fenders, windshields, and lights, to make the car more **aerodynamic**. When the race was over, the drivers replaced the parts on their cars and drove home.

In 1937, a group called the Southern California Timing Association (SCTA) was formed, and drag racing, also called hot rodding, got more serious. The SCTA decided to start having an ambulance service at races in case of an accident. The group also created a points system to determine who would be the champion of a series of races.

In 1949, the president of the SCTA, Wally Parks, became the editor of a new magazine called *Hot Rod*. One day a reader wrote to Parks and asked why there wasn't a national organization devoted to hot rodding. Parks and the magazine publishers liked the idea, and they formed the National Hot Rod Association (NHRA), with Parks as president. In 1953, the first city-sponsored, NHRA-organized race was held in Pomona, California. Today, the first and last races of the NHRA season are held at the Pomona track. Although there are other drag racing organizations, the NHRA is the biggest.

Since race classes rotate throughout the day, spectators can spend the entire day watching different races from the grandstands. But many fans, once they have seen their favorite team or race class, often go to the pit area to get an up-close view of their teams in action. Race teams usually have 90 minutes between passes, or rounds, before they have to race again. During this time, the pits are a flurry of activity as teams prepare the cars for the next race. Unlike other forms of racing, in drag racing fans are allowed in the pit area and can watch their favorite teams at work. Many times, a driver will sign autographs while his team works on the car.

THE FORCE IS WITH THEM

One of the most popular drag racing drivers is John Force. A 13-time national champion, Force is probably the most entertaining driver in racing today. He races a Funny Car and is always cracking jokes and telling stories.

One of Force's two crew chiefs is Bernie Fedderly. He has been on the team since 1992 but has been involved in racing for much longer than that. As a crew chief, Fedderly handles the mechanical aspects of running the team, as well as managing the crew of the six race teams that are a part of John Force Racing.

Funny Car race hero John Force, shown at his showroom in Yorba Linda, California, talks about life in the fast lane.

When the team isn't racing, Fedderly is in the team's Yorba Linda, California, office by 8:30 A.M. Fedderly handles all the paperwork for all the teams and coordinates traveling details such as hotels and transportation, to get all the teams and their equipment to the next race. He also talks with the other crew chiefs about the team's strategy or new projects. During the winter, days are especially long because all the equipment is at the shop being rebuilt. It is not unusual for the crew to work 10 hours a day during that time.

Traveling to the races is a big production for the Force team. In 2005, the team ran three Funny Cars: one Top Alcohol Dragster and two SuperComp race cars. It took 28 people to get all the support vehicles and race equipment to every race. Eight big rig trucks, five support vehicles, a bus, and a trailer travel to each race.

Funny Cars each have eight crewmembers assigned to them, plus a crew chief and a driver. Crew chief Austin Coil works primarily on Force's car. Chief John Medlen works mainly on his son Eric Medlen's car, and chief Jimmy Prock works on Robert Hight's car. Fedderly floats between all of them but works mainly on Force's car.

Pit stops in drag racing aren't as fast as they are in other forms of racing, because the dragster crew has a lot of work to do on the cars between rounds. In just 90 minutes, the team jacks up the car, drains the oil, and downloads information about the last round from a computer on board the car. The crew chief analyzes the computer data and decides on a strategy for the next round. Meanwhile, the crew inspects and repairs or cleans most of the parts on the engine, including the supercharger, valves and springs, cylinder heads, engine bearings, and crankshaft. They replace the rods and pistons and reassemble the engine. New sparkplugs, oil, and an oil filter are added. Once the engine work is complete, the engine is started and the crew makes adjustments and checks it for leaks.

If the car is damaged during one of the rounds, things become hectic for the pit crew. The team always has spare engine parts in their trailer, as well as an extra body for each car. The team must be prepared for any problem, because if the car is not able to advance to the next round of competition, the team's chances at the championship are in question.

The most difficult problem a pit crew faces is if the car catches on fire during a run. Damage from a fire will often put a team out of the race, but, if the team is well prepared, they can repair the car and continue to race. In cases of fire, the crew must also change most of the rubber hoses because they are often damaged by heat. There are many hoses on these vehicles, and replacing them is a long and dull job.

In 1992 at the Mid-South Nationals in Memphis, Tennessee, John Force had a bad accident. It was during the semifinal round of competition, and his car caught on fire. Because of this accident, the team felt it was necessary to make safety improvements to protect Funny Car drivers. The team played a big part in developing a fire shield, a piece on the **cowl** that protects the driver from the engine during a fire. They also helped develop a fresh air system that allows the driver to breathe in a fire. The fresh air system is required for all NHRA drivers today, and many other racers use the fire shield on their cars, too.

Being a member of a winning team is fun, but it is also very demanding. During the race season, Force's crew is on the road more than they are at home. Crewmembers take turns taking breaks to go home, and sometimes they bring their families to the track with them during race weekends. Fedderly has a slightly freer schedule because, as crew chief, he usually flies to the races instead of driving like most of the crew. Still, Fedderly usually flies to a race on a Wednesday and doesn't return until the following Monday evening. That's about 140 days of travel every year.

Although the schedule is demanding, many people still want to get one of the spots on the team. Fedderly admits that getting a position on a race team is pretty difficult for someone new to racing. In general, team owners look for people who have a special skill, such as computer training, truck driving, machining, or fabrication. One of the best ways to get a job with a team is to apply for a job that does not require mechanical skills, such as driving one of the transport trucks. Then it is possible to work hard and get experience for a mechanical job. To Fedderly, hiring a new employee who has a college degree is important, but not nearly as important as real-world experience. "You must be a team player and have good people skills," says Fedderly. "You have to be able to [set yourself apart] from hundreds of other people who want a job too."

4

ENDURANCE RACING

Modern-day car racing is filled with rules. Most kinds of car racing, however, didn't start out that way. A group of people who loved to drive fast got together to race in a variety of places, from the cow pastures of early stock car racing to the dry lakebeds of early drag racing. Now races are put together by governing organizations, such as NASCAR or NHRA, and they have many race officials who oversee every race.

Although many officials have many different duties, all officials have one main goal: to make sure that racing is safe. The organizations' rules protect the drivers, crew, and spectators from accidents on the track. Another reason to have so many rules is to keep racing fair, so that everyone has an equal chance to win.

THE LONG HAUL

Endurance racing has the most rules of any kind of car racing. In endurance racing, a race team runs one car for 12 or 24 hours straight, stopping only to switch drivers, refuel, or repair the car. This type of racing is hard on the race car and on the drivers.

Endurance racing is an international sport, and teams from all over the world travel to many different countries to compete in these long races. In endurance racing, the winning team is the one that has driven the most miles at the end of the 12- or 24-hour time period. Among famous endurance races are the 12 Hours of Sebring, 24 Hours of Daytona, and 24 Hours of Le Mans. Each race is run on a road course, which includes left and right turns and **straightaways**. Sometimes these races are run on public roads that have been blocked off to regular traffic during the race. At times, endurance races are run on racetracks designed especially for road racing. These tracks are used for other road racing events in addition to endurance races.

Bob Berridge of Great Britain maneuvers the curves during the 24 Hours of Le Mans in Le Mans, France, in June 2006.

One reason endurance racing seems to have more rules than other types of racing is that there are several different organizations that oversee different races. Each organization has different rules, and teams have to follow these different rules at every race.

The American Le Mans Series (ALMS) oversees the 12 Hours of Sebring race in Sebring, Florida. Founded in 1999 by Don Panoz, ALMS hosts a series of endurance racing events. The events are modeled after the 24 Hours of Le Mans, a race in France where the competitors race on public roads (which have been closed to other drivers) for 24 hours straight. There are four classes of competition and all four classes compete on the track at the same time. Each class has a different type of vehicle, with different mechanical and design requirements. Teams are organized by car manufacturers, as well as by **privateers**.

ALMS races are run using the same rules that are used for the 24 Hours of Le Mans. These rules were created by the Automobile Club de l'Ouest (ACO), the French organization that oversees the 24 Hours of Le Mans. All ALMS races, however, are **sanctioned** and organized by the International Motor Sports Association (IMSA), which oversees several road racing series in the United States. Teams that race regularly in ALMS events get special consideration when the ACO is choosing the 48 teams it will invite to compete in the 24 Hours of Le Mans. Fifteen ALMS teams were invited to participate in the 2005 24 Hours of Le Mans, based on their racing successes the year before.

The longest of the ALMS races is the 12 Hours of Sebring, held at Sebring International Raceway. The

PANOZ'S HISTORY

Don Panoz, founder of the American Le Mans Series, has been involved in motor sports since the mid-1990s. He is the owner of the Panoz Motor Sports Group, which includes a racing school, three road-racing tracks, and the Panoz Racing Series. He also owns Elan Motor Sports Technologies, which builds race cars and engines. One of the divisions of Elan Motor Sports, Panoz G Force, was responsible for building the framework for the vehicle that won the 2003 Indianapolis 500. Panoz got his start in motor sports due to his son Danny's project as an auto manufacturer under a company called Panoz Auto Development. When the Panoz GTR-1 began racing in 1997, Don Panoz realized that American sports car racing was in trouble and he led an effort to bring it back to world-class status.

Sebring track is located in central Florida, a few miles north of Lake Okeechobee. The track was originally a military base for B-17 bomber training. The maze of airplane runways and service roads was converted into a racecourse that has been called an American version of the 24 Hours of Le Mans. The course is 5.2 miles of pretzel-shaped twists and turns that are known to cause many mechanical problems for the race cars. Drivers frequently race down the straightaways at faster than 150 miles per hour at Sebring, only to be forced to slow down to enter sharp curves. Slowing down quickly is not easy. The car skids and sways under the strain as the tires squeal in an effort to slow down. All this strain means that the car could break apart at any time and need to pull into the pits for repairs.

CORVETTE TEAM SPIRIT

One team that competes in road racing, including 12- and 24-hour endurance races, is the Corvette Racing team. The Chevrolet Corvette first began racing in 1956 at the 24 Hours of Le Mans. In 2004, the Corvette Racing team earned its fourth-straight manufacturer's championship, in addition to winning its class. There are two cars on the Corvette Racing team. Program manager Doug Fehan has been with the team since 1996. He is responsible for every decision regarding the team. It is up to Fehan to make sure all members of the team, such as engine tuners and aerodynamic specialists, are working on their part of the race car and are working together.

24-hour endurance racing tests the limits of the car and crew and requires nighttime pit stops.

Audi Sport North America drivers change places during a pit stop in the final practice before the 12 Hours of Sebring race in Sebring, Florida, in March 2006.

During the race, Fehan wears a headset and monitors all the decisions the Corvette Racing team makes. If he disagrees with them, or if they are unsure, Fehan makes the final decision about changes to the car or the race strategy. There are about 30 people in the Corvette Racing pit during the race. Two are drivers waiting for their turns behind the wheel. Unlike other forms of racing, there are multiple drivers for the same car in endurance racing.

There are four people who go over the wall to do work on the car, such as changing the tires. There are helpers who assist those who go over the wall by carrying tires or getting fuel. One person is dedicated to helping the current driver out of the car and getting the new driver into the car. Endurance racing drivers usually change places at every pit stop.

On the morning of race day, Fehan and key members of the crew discuss the pit stop strategy for that race. "The most important thing in any race is your pit stop strategy under the caution flag," says Fehan. At one race in 2004, the difference between first and second place was determined by the speed of the pit stop.

That race was the last of the season at the Mazda Raceway Laguna Seca in Monterey, California. The two Corvette cars had been doing well all season and it was almost sure that they were going to finish first and second in their class. No one knew which car would finish first. At this race, both cars had been in the lead at different times, and, on the last pit stop, both cars came into the pits at almost exactly the same time. Fehan was there, watching, as the pit crews for both teams sprang into action.

"They knew that the result of the race was in their hands," says Fehan. "I watched them jump into action and how they were choreographed with every step. When the number 3 car got out [of the pits] first, the

The number 3 car of the Corvette Racing team gets serviced during the pit stop that sealed its victory in the final race at Mazda Raceway Laguna Seca in Monterey, California, in 2004.

crew was jubilant—they knew they'd won the race and the championship."

Donny Atkins works in the pits with Fehan. Atkins's job is to install each car's tiny sensors that collect information. The sensors monitor items such as brake temperature and engine performance. The information is recorded in a computer in the car and also sent instantly to a computer Atkins has in the pits.

During the race, Atkins studies the information from every sensor on both cars, while other engineers watch only one car for one aspect, such as the engine performance. "I regularly talk with the other [engineers] to determine suggestions, such as our fuel strategy, which we then recommend to the crew chief," says Atkins.

Pit stops at Le Mans have more rules than those at other endurance races. In fact, compared to the lightning-fast stops in Winston Cup or Indy Car racing, these pit stops seem to be in slow motion. When the car first comes into the pit area, the driver is required to stop the car completely and shut off the engine before any work can begin. No one else is allowed to work on the car while it is being refueled. After refueling, four mechanics can begin their work. If a major part of the car breaks down, it is not uncommon for teams to spend an hour or more in the pits.

The 24 Hours of Le Mans is considered the most demanding of all the endurance races. It is made up of a little more than eight miles of public roads with tunnels, dips, and bridges in addition to its famous twists and turns. The town of Le Mans is located 130 miles southwest of Paris, France, and it is filled with cloth factories. Every year in June, the town roars to life with some of the most spectacular cars in the world, which gather there to compete in the thrilling but grueling race.

One of the keys to winning any type of race is to have a well-built car that doesn't break down on the track. Although this is important in any kind of car racing, it is especially important to those competing in endurance races. The crew must be sure that each part is of the highest quality so it can survive the strain of being used for 12 or 24 hours straight. For example, during the 24 Hours of Le Mans, the average winning car travels more than 3,000 miles—the distance from New York City to Los Angeles—or even farther.

At the 24 Hours of Le Mans in 2004, the Corvette team encountered many obstacles, but eventually its two cars placed first and second in their class. One car suffered a popped tire early into the race, causing much damage to the car and bringing the team down one driver. As a result, the remaining two drivers drove for more than 10 hours each in a true test of endurance. The accident was just one of several the two cars experienced. Still, both the Corvettes came out winners in the end, beating out all the other cars in the class.

"Before the end of the race, everyone was trying to pitch in and get the cars back on the track," says Atkins. "When the two Corvettes came through the finish line, I cried, I was so happy."

Fehan says that the 24 hours of Le Mans is both the most exciting and the most challenging experience the team has all year. "It's like the Superbowl of racing times 10. The best teams in the world are there. When you see the two cars coming toward the finish line, it is overwhelming. . . . We've won it three times and it never gets to be ordinary."

5

OFF-ROAD RACING

Off-road racing is tough on a driver's body as well as the car. Off-road drivers must be in good physical condition. They must endure the endless bumps of an uneven course and the scorching heat that comes from the engine of a car that has been running for hours. This kind of racing is a test of **stamina** for both driver and vehicle, and stamina is a key part of winning races.

An off-road racecourse covers many different types of terrain, such as dirt roads, dry riverbeds, rocks, canyons, tidal pools near beaches, and even mountain trails. Because of the different types of terrain, off-road racers drive at many different speeds during the race. A driver may travel at only 20 miles per hour through a very difficult section, and then speed up to faster than 100 miles per hour when the course is less dangerous.

Off-road racecourses are mapped out by race organizers and marked with flags, called course markers. Every car that participates in an off-road race carries two people. Usually the two people take turns driving a portion of the race, and the person who is not driving navigates.

Veteran off-road racer Rod Hall mastered the extreme racing conditions of the 2006 Blue Water Resort & Casino Parker 425 to finish first in his class. The Parker 425 race winds through the harsh Arizona desert along the Colorado River.

The navigator makes sure that the car stays on the course by using the course map and watching out for the course markers. Good navigation is important because sometimes the course can be especially dangerous in some places. In fact, some off-road racers have been known to drive off cliffs because they couldn't see where they were going.

Racing on all that uneven ground is very hard on the racers. The race vehicle is speeding forward, but it's also bouncing up and down. Plus, the noise is incredible. Every part of the vehicle groans and screams under the pressure. Things rattle and shake and it is nearly impossible to hear anything or anyone.

BEATING OTHERS AT THE BAJA

The oldest and most famous of all off-road races is the Tecate SCORE Baja 1000. The Baja 1000 takes place in November, and begins in Ensenada, Baja California, Mexico. This race usually starts in Ensenada, makes a giant loop through Baja California, and ends back in Ensenada where it began. Depending on how the race organizers lay it out, the course ranges from 700 to more 1,000 miles long. Many years ago, in the early days of the race, the course started in Ensenada and finished in La Paz, close to the end of the Baja California peninsula. Today the race organizers skip the loop race every three or four years and hold the race from Ensenada to La Paz instead, like in the old days.

When organizers use the straight route from Ensenada to La Paz, it costs more than twice as much as the loop course. Race teams can expect to spend double the amount of money when running the straight course. Because both amateurs and professionals race in the Baja 1000, using the straight route every year would mean that not as many teams could afford to participate.

The first known recorded run was in 1962 when Dave Elkins and Bill Robertson Jr. timed their trip from Tijuana to La Paz on a pair of Honda 250 motorcycles. It took Elkins 39 hours and 54 minutes, while his partner took almost an hour longer. To prove that they had completed their run in the time they said, the two went to the telegraph office in Tijuana and had a sheet of paper stamped with the time there. When they arrived in La Paz, they had the same sheet stamped with the time at the telegraph office there.

PATTERNED POSITIONING

Off-road racing teams use a Global Positioning System (GPS) to ensure that they don't get lost. A GPS is a small computer that tells the driver and navigator where they are. The GPS sends a signal to a satellite, which determines where the signal is coming from. Then it sends the information back to the GPS, marking the spot on the map.

There are special GPS units designed for off-road driving. A vehicle driving through the desert will kick up a lot of dirt. This can create a cloud of dust around the vehicle, making it hard for the driver and navigator to see. An off-road racing GPS allows the racers to mark the course map with symbols to show their pit stops as well as dangerous areas, such as big rocks or steep cliffs.

The company Chevrolet heard about the motorcycle racers' efforts. They hired a famous car builder named Bill Stroppe to build a fleet of trucks to do the same thing. When all the trucks made it to La Paz, advertising campaigns called their accomplishment "the toughest run under the sun."

Before long, in 1967, the National Off-Road Racing Association (NORRA) was formed and the Mexican 1000 was born. The Mexican 1000 eventually became known as the Baja 1000. From 1967 to 1973, the Baja 1000 ran from Ensenada to La Paz every year except 1972, when it started in Mexicali. The race has, however, experienced some bumps in the road. In 1973, Mexican officials took back NORRA's privileges to stage races in Baja. The next year, 1974, the race was canceled because of a serious gasoline shortage in the country at that time. But that wasn't the end of the Baja 1000.

Zero visibility is the result when Chad Hall plows through silt in his H1 during the 2006 Vegas-to-Reno race. Silt—powdered limestone deposited by rivers—is left behind when rivers dry up. It has the consistency of freshly fallen snow, and drivers drive through it in much the same way.

After the gasoline crisis was over, the northern Mexican state of Baja California invited a group, SCORE International, to host the race in 1975. SCORE mapped out the current loop route that begins and ends in Ensenada and has organized the race ever since. Today SCORE can run the race on whichever route they choose. In 2004, the Baja 1000 ran on the straight course, beginning in Ensenada and ending in La Paz. It was 1,016.3 miles long. Nearly 300 vehicles from 31 U.S. states and 10 countries competed in that race.

At the beginning of the race, one vehicle leaves the start line every 30 seconds as the fans cheer it on. And they're off, for 15 hours and more, on one of the most demanding races in the world. The teams blast off down the canyon, the noises of their engines revving at full speed, the sound echoing off the walls. Some of the more powerful vehicles spray gravel onto the hoods of cars parked as far away as two blocks. In 2004, the winner of the race was Steve Hengeveld, who completed the race in 15 hours, 57 minutes, and 37 seconds on his Honda motorcycle.

The driver and navigator are alone much of the time during the race. Vehicles called chase trucks use less demanding routes to follow the racers. The race car stays in radio contact with the chase trucks and pit crew. The navigator keeps track of the vehicle's position using a Global Positioning System (GPS). Every few miles, he radios in their position so the crew can keep track of the vehicle. Many times during the course, the race vehicle is out of radio range (such as when it is traveling through a canyon), so it is important that the crew knows where the race vehicle is as often as possible. If the vehicle breaks down, the crew must be able to find it quickly so only a little of the precious race time is lost.

Rod Hall is a veteran Baja 1000 racer. He has competed in every race since the first one in 1967 and continued even as he entered his sixties. Hall is the only person who raced on four wheels in the first Baja 1000 and is still racing today. Hall has won in his class a record 18 times and, in 1969, was the first one out of all the classes to cross the finish line.

Hall's two sons, Chad and Josh, also race and are involved in the family business, Rod Hall Products. When the Halls are racing, they drive Hummers.

When preparing for a race, a team of two people must work full-time for at least 30 days to prepare. The crew

Rod Hall, seen inside his H3 Hummer, clearly enjoys his work. In November 2006, he finished the Baja 1000 first in his class—three days shy of his sixtyninth birthday.

checks over every part of the vehicle. Because teams aren't allowed to reinforce the stock vehicles, many items have to be replaced after a race. Suspension pieces, such as crossmembers and a-arms, are inspected for cracks and other damage. The crew takes almost the whole vehicle apart and inspects every piece carefully. Sometimes old parts are replaced with new ones. Other times, the same part is reinstalled.

Sometimes during a race, a part breaks down on the vehicle and the team is too far away from the pit crew. In these instances the driver and navigator must fix the car by themselves. The Hummer carries many spare parts in case of such an emergency. The crew stocks the vehicle with parts that the car needs to move, such as ball joints,

The Hall racing family includes *(from left)* youngest son Chad, who drives the H1; oldest son Josh, who drives the H2; and dad Rod, who drives the H3.

fuses, electrical wire, steering parts, a fan belt, and spare tires. Parts that are too big or heavy are left behind. The team also carries all the extra fluids they need for the vehicle, including extra oil, transmission fluid, and water for the radiator. Being prepared is important because, just like in other kinds of racing, the speed of repairs during the race can often determine the winner.

When preparing for the Baja 1000, drivers have the opportunity to drive the course in advance. This is called a prerun. It enables teams to learn the route and look for dangerous areas, such as big holes. They use their GPS computers to note certain landmarks and dangerous spots along the course. During the race, this computer helps guide them. The prerun allows the drivers to determine where their chase vehicles should be placed. The Halls have five or six support vehicles stationed at various places along the course to help them if their car breaks down.

When the Halls go on their prerun, they take the same model Hummer that they will race—an H1, H2, or H3 that has been modified only slightly for the course. Because the prerun is done at slower speeds than the race, they do not need other race equipment in their vehicle. They do leave in certain items, such as air-conditioning and windows, so they are more comfortable. In the race truck, they remove those items to help reduce the weight of the vehicle, which helps them go faster.

During the Baja 1000, there are pit stops roughly every 125 miles. Since the pit crew can't see where the team car is on the course, the driver radios ahead to tell the crew how far away he is from the pit area. Then the crew can get ready for his arrival. When the Halls' Hummers enter the pits, a crewmember pumps 40 to 50 gallons of fuel into each of the cars while other members of the team check the tires. The pit crew checks under the hood and under each vehicle, looking for any areas that are wet. Because it is dry and dusty in the desert, wet spots usually mean there is a leak somewhere on the vehicle.

More often than not, something will go wrong with the vehicle when the driver is nowhere near the pit area. It has happened many times to the Halls. In 2004, Josh Hall was driving a Hummer H2 in the Baja 1000. At the 600-mile mark, he hit a washed-out patch of the course and the vehicle flipped over. Fortunately, the pit crew was in the chase truck only about 10 miles away. They arrived quickly and helped Josh and his dad, who was codriving,

Chad Hall's H1 receives attention during a pit stop in the 2006 Vegas-to-Reno race, the longest off-road race in the United States.

fix the vehicle. The accident cost them a lot of extra time and they ended up finishing in fourth place in their class. Fortunately, the winner in that class was Chad Hall and his codriver, Mike Winkel, who finished the race about eight hours ahead of the father-son Hall team.

In order to win, or even to finish a Baja 1000 race, the driver must know not to push himself or the vehicle too far. Rod Hall says that knowing his vehicle's ability and being a disciplined driver are the qualities that got him into the winner's circle so many times. The Baja 1000 is a much more intense race today than it was when it first started. Discipline and stamina help drivers reach the finish line, and just finishing one of the toughest races in the world is certainly an accomplishment.

CHRONOLOGY

1923 The 24 Hours of Le Mans race is held in Le Mans, France for the first time.

1932 First drag races are held on dry lakebeds.

1937 Southern California Timing Association (SCTA) is formed.

1934 Bill France visits Daytona Beach, Florida, and is fascinated by stock car racing on the beach there.

1947 National Association for Stock Car Automobile Racing (NASCAR) is formed.

1948 First NASCAR race is held in Daytona Beach, Florida.

1949 Wally Parks, SCTA president, becomes editor of *Hot Rod* magazine; National Hot Rod Association (NHRA) is formed.

1953 First NHRA drag race is held in Pomona, California.

1955 Worst accident in racing history: 80 spectators are killed when Pierre Levegh's Mercedes-Benz 300 SLR crashes and becomes airborne at the 24 Hours of Le Mans; Levegh also dies in the accident.

1960 Wood Brothers Racing discovers they have an advantage over the competition by reducing the time spent at a pit stop.

1962 Dave Elkins and Bill Robertson Jr. time their trip from Tijuana, Mexico, to La Paz, Mexico, on a pair of Honda 250 motorcycles; Chevrolet later hires Bill Stroppe to build a fleet of trucks to do the same thing as publicity for the company.

1967   National Off-Road Racing Association (NORRA) holds first Mexican 1000, which will eventually become known as the Baja 1000.

1973   Mexican officials revoke NORRA's privileges to stage off-road races in Baja California, Mexico.

1975   SCORE International takes over organizing the Baja 1000, which becomes a loop race beginning and ending in Ensenada.

1978   John Force races in his first Funny Car race.

1979   Mexican officials restore racing privilege, allowing the Baja 1000 to run from Ensenada to La Paz.

1994   John Force becomes the Funny Car driver with the most wins in the history of the sport.

1995   NASCAR launches Craftsman Truck Series.

2004   John Force wins his thirteenth NHRA Funny Car championship; Corvette Racing wins the GTS Class in the 24 Hours of Le Mans.

2006   John Force wins his fourteenth NHRA Funny Car championship; Force and his family star in the A&E Television reality TV series *Driving Force*.

GLOSSARY

Aerodynamic—Designed with round edges to increase speed and lessen the amount of fuel needed to drive.

Burnout—When a driver spins the rear wheels of a drag-racing car, causing the rubber to heat up and burn.

Caution flag—A yellow flag that warns the drivers of a problem on the track, such as an accident. In NASCAR racing, drivers must hold their positions and not pass other cars when the caution flag is out.

Cowl—The forward part of the body of a motor vehicle supporting the rear of the hood and the windshield and housing the pedals and instrument panel.

Dry-Hop—The process of accelerating a drag racing car rapidly for a short distance, which readies the car for the race.

Endurance racing—Long-distance car racing, one of the most demanding of all types of racing on both the car and the driver.

Jackman—The job title for the person who is responsible for raising and lowering the car in order to change the tires during a NASCAR racing pit stop.

Privateer—A race team owned by an individual or group of individuals.

Sanctioned—Allowed to happen; the decision is usually made by an official person or group.

Stamina—Physical or moral strength to withstand illness or hardship.

Straightaway—A course or portion of a course without a curve or a turn.

Supercharger—A device that pumps air into the engine in order to increase the power of the engine.

Traction—The adhesive friction of a body on a surface, such as a tire on a road.

BIBLIOGRAPHY

Addison, Nicole. Personal interview, March 13, 2005.

Breslauer, Ken, and Dan Gurney. *Sebring: The Official History of America's Great Sports Car Race.* Phoenix, Ariz.: David Bull Publishing, 1996.

Burt, William. *Stock Car Race Shop: Design and Construction of a NASCAR Stock Car.* St. Paul, Minn.: MBI Publishing, 2001.

Dykehouse, Sara. Personal interview, March 23, 2005.

Fedderly, Bernie. Personal interview, March 14, 2005.

Fehan, Doug. Personal interview, March 23, 2005.

Johnstone, Mike. *NASCAR: The Need For Speed.* Minneapolis, Minn.: Lerner Sports, 2002.

Laban, Brian. *Le Mans 24 Hours.* Osceloa, Wisc.: Motorbooks, 2001.

National Hot Rod Association. *The Fast Lane: The History of NHRA Drag Racing.* New York: Regan Books, 2001

Rich, Ronda. *My Life in the Pits.* New York: HarperEntertainment, 2002.

Sexton, Susan. *Drag Racing: Attacking The Green.* Des Moines, Iowa: Perfection Learning, 2003.

FURTHER READING

Buckley, James, Jr. *Life In the Pits: Twenty Seconds That Make the Difference.* Chanhassen, Minn: The Child's World, 2003.

Genat, Robert. *American Drag Racing.* Osceloa, Wisc.: Motorbooks, 2001.

Hammond, Jeff, and Gregg Norman. *Real Men Work in the Pits: A Life in NASCAR Racing.* New York: Rodale Books, 2005.

Laban, Brian. *Le Mans 24 Hours.* Osceloa, Wisc.: Motorbooks, 2001.

Mead, Sue. *Off-Road Racing.* New York: Chelsea House, 2005.

Moity, Christian, and Jean-Marc Tessedre. *24 Hours of Le Mans 2004.* Paris: Chronosports, 2005.

Woods, Bob. *NASCAR Pit Pass: Behind the Scenes of NASCAR* (NASCAR Middle Grade Book). Pleasantville, N.Y.: Reader's Digest, 2005.

WEB SITES

www.americanlemans.com
Official Web site of the American Le Mans endurance racing series.

www.corvetteracing.com
Web site of the Corvette Racing team.

www.hengeracing.com
Web site of Steve Hengeveld, the overall winner of the 2004 Baja 1000.

www.lemans.org
Official Web site of the Automobile Club de l'Ouest, the French organization that oversees the 24 Hours of Le Mans race.

www.jacksprague.com
Web site of Jack Sprague and the No. 16 NASCAR Craftsman Truck team.

www.johnforce.com
Web site of John Force and his teammates.

www.nascar.com
Official Web site for the National Association of Stock Car Auto Racing. Provides information about all classes of racing that NASCAR oversees, as well as drivers and sponsors associated with this organization. Extensive search function for news, drivers, teams, and sponsors.

www.nascar.about.com
About.com's guide to everything about NASCAR racing; Includes section for fans new to NASCAR racing.

www.nhra.com
Official Web site for the National Hot Rod Association. Provides information about all drag racing classes it oversees as well as drivers and sponsors associated with this organization.

www.racingone.com
Web site devoted to the news from all different types of professional racing.

www.score-international.com
Official Web site for the organization that oversees the Baja 1000.

www.winkelhummer.com
HUMMER dealership partially owned by Hall family. Features a section on the Rod Hall Racing team.

PICTURE CREDITS

INDEX

ABOUT THE AUTHOR

TARA BAUKUS MELLO is a freelance automotive writer. During her 20 years as a writer, she has published more than 3,700 articles in newspapers and magazines. Baukus Mello is the author of *Tony Stewart, Rusty Wallace, Mark Martin, The Pit Crew, Stunt Driving,* and *Danica Patrick,* all part of Chelsea House's RACE CAR LEGENDS: COLLECTOR'S EDITION series. A graduate of Harvard University, she lives in Southern California, where she cruises the streets in her 1932 Ford pickup street rod that she built with her father.